You're
MAGIC

summersdale

YOU'RE MAGIC

An Hachette UK Company
www.hachette.co.uk

Summersdale Publishers Ltd
Part of Octopus Publishing Group Limited
Carmelite House
50 Victoria Embankment
LONDON
EC4Y 0DZ
UK

www.summersdale.com

Printed and bound in China

ISBN: 978-1-78783-227-5

Substantial discounts on bulk quantities of Summersdale books are available to corporations, professional associations and other organizations. For details contact general enquiries: telephone: +44 (0) 1243 771107 or email: enquiries@summersdale.com.

TO ..... Julie

FROM ..... Peter
       & Lois

Thou, fresh
piece of excellent
witchcraft.

WILLIAM SHAKESPEARE

DON'T EVER LET A
SOUL IN THE WORLD
TELL YOU THAT YOU
CAN'T BE EXACTLY
WHO YOU ARE.

LADY GAGA

YOU'RE

aura-some

YOU ARE MAGNIFICENT BEYOND MEASURE, PERFECT IN YOUR IMPERFECTIONS AND WONDERFULLY MADE.

ABIOLA ABRAMS

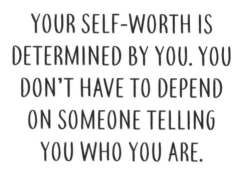

YOUR SELF-WORTH IS
DETERMINED BY YOU. YOU
DON'T HAVE TO DEPEND
ON SOMEONE TELLING
YOU WHO YOU ARE.

BEYONCÉ

THOSE WHO
DON'T BELIEVE
IN MAGIC WILL
NEVER FIND IT.

ROALD DAHL

Never dull
your shine for
somebody else.

TYRA BANKS

THE QUESTION
ISN'T WHO'S GOING
TO LET ME; IT'S WHO'S
GOING TO STOP ME.

AYN RAND

EVERYTHING

about

YOU IS

hex-cellent

THE UNIVERSE IS FULL OF MAGICAL THINGS, PATIENTLY WAITING FOR OUR WITS TO GROW SHARPER.

EDEN PHILLPOTTS

I promise
you that each
and every one of
you is made to be
who you are.

SELENA GOMEZ

THERE IS MAGIC,
BUT YOU HAVE TO BE
THE MAGICIAN. YOU
HAVE TO MAKE THE
MAGIC HAPPEN.

SIDNEY SHELDON

YOU
ARE SO
powerful

IF WE DID ALL
THE THINGS WE ARE
CAPABLE OF DOING,
WE WOULD LITERALLY
ASTOUND OURSELVES.

THOMAS EDISON

BE BRAVE ENOUGH TO BE YOUR TRUE SELF.

QUEEN LATIFAH

THE PERSON WHO
SAYS IT CANNOT BE
DONE SHOULD NOT
INTERRUPT THE PERSON
WHO IS DOING IT.

ANONYMOUS

We will always
tend to fulfil our
own expectations
of ourselves.

BRIAN TRACY

Let nothing
bind you in the
world other than
your highest
inner truth.

EMMA HERWEGH

YOU LIFT THE

spirits

OF THOSE AROUND

you

ALL OUR DREAMS CAN COME TRUE IF WE HAVE THE COURAGE TO PURSUE THEM.

WALT DISNEY

YOU... HAVE TO
FOLLOW YOUR
OWN STAR.

BOB DYLAN

YOU'RE

abraca-

FAB-ra

NOTHING
CAN DIM
THE LIGHT
WHICH SHINES
FROM WITHIN.

MAYA ANGELOU

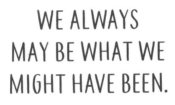

WE ALWAYS
MAY BE WHAT WE
MIGHT HAVE BEEN.

ADELAIDE ANNE PROCTER

Life itself is
the most
wonderful
fairy tale.

HANS CHRISTIAN ANDERSEN

YOU'RE

tarot-tally

BRILLIANT

Sometimes
it's worth risking
it all for a dream
only you can see.

MEGAN RAPINOE

REAL MAGIC IS NOT ABOUT GAINING POWER OVER OTHERS: IT IS ABOUT GAINING POWER OVER YOURSELF.

ROSEMARY ELLEN GUILEY

YOU'RE SO *awesome* IT MUST BE *sorcery!*

NOTHING SPLENDID
HAS EVER BEEN
ACHIEVED EXCEPT
BY THOSE WHO
DARED BELIEVE THAT
SOMETHING INSIDE
THEM WAS SUPERIOR
TO CIRCUMSTANCE.

BRUCE FAIRCHILD BARTON

Never be
limited by other
people's limited
imaginations.

MAE JEMISON

RIDE THE ENERGY
OF YOUR OWN
UNIQUE SPIRIT.

GABRIELLE ROTH

THERE IS NO MAGIC
WHEN ONE NO
LONGER BELIEVES.

HILDA LEWIS

If you give
people a chance,
they shine.

BILLY CONNOLLY

YOU'RE

-=- *divine* -=-

PUT ASIDE ALL
EXCUSES AND
REMEMBER: YOU
ARE CAPABLE.

ZIG ZIGLAR

I THINK
WE CAN ALL
ACTUALLY
BE MORE
SUPERHUMAN
THAN WE THINK
WE CAN.

EDDIE IZZARD

TO ACCOMPLISH
GREAT THINGS,
WE MUST NOT
ONLY ACT, BUT
ALSO DREAM;
NOT ONLY PLAN,
BUT ALSO
BELIEVE.

ANATOLE FRANCE

YOU HAVE

=*magic*=

IN YOUR EYES

Stay strong
and be yourself!
It's the best
thing you
can be.

CARA DELEVINGNE

EVERY DAY
HOLDS THE
POSSIBILITY OF
A MIRACLE.

ELIZABETH DAVID

THERE ARE BEAUTIFUL MOMENTS OF MAGIC IN EVERYONE'S LIFE.

PENÉLOPE CRUZ

FOLLOW YOUR
INNER MOONLIGHT;
DON'T HIDE THE
MADNESS.

ALLEN GINSBERG

Feet, what
do I need you
for when I have
wings to fly?

FRIDA KAHLO

YOU'RE A

blessing,

NEVER A

curse!

THE POWER
OF THOUGHT,
THE MAGIC OF
THE MIND!

LORD BYRON

BE SURE WHAT
YOU WANT AND
BE SURE ABOUT
YOURSELF...
YOU HAVE TO
BELIEVE IN
YOURSELF AND
BE STRONG.

ADRIANA LIMA

YOU HAVE

great

AND POWERFUL

portent-ial

TO ACHIEVE GREATNESS,
START WHERE YOU ARE,
USE WHAT YOU HAVE AND
DO WHAT YOU CAN.

ARTHUR ASHE

Trust yourself;
believe that you
have a unique
destiny to fulfil.

CANDY PAULL

IF MY MIND CAN
CONCEIVE IT
AND MY HEART
CAN BELIEVE
IT – THEN I CAN
ACHIEVE IT.

JESSE JACKSON

There's a bit of magic in everything.

LOU REED

PUT YOUR FUTURE
IN GOOD HANDS
— YOUR OWN.

MARK VICTOR HANSEN

YOU ARE
extraordinary

FIRST, THINK.
SECOND, BELIEVE.
THIRD, DREAM. AND
FINALLY, DARE.

WALT DISNEY

Follow your dreams. They know the way.

KOBI YAMADA

WITCHERY
IS MERELY
A WORD
FOR WHAT
WE ARE ALL
CAPABLE OF.

CHARLES DE LINT

WE ARE MAGIC.
IT IS MAGIC THAT WE'RE
WALKING AROUND.

DONOVAN

I BELIEVE
IN MYSELF,
EVEN MY MOST
DELICATE
INTANGIBLE
FEELINGS.

MARILYN MONROE

BET YOU
DIDN'T
ex-spectre
SO MANY
compliments

WHEN YOU'RE
TRUE TO WHO YOU
ARE, AMAZING
THINGS HAPPEN.

DEBORAH NORVILLE

Magic lies in
challenging what
seems impossible.

CAROL MOSELEY BRAUN

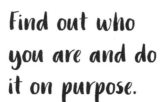

Find out who
you are and do
it on purpose.

DOLLY PARTON

YOU ARE
spellbinding

HIDE NOT YOUR
TALENTS, THEY FOR
USE WERE MADE.
WHAT'S A SUNDIAL
IN THE SHADE?

BENJAMIN FRANKLIN

BELIEVE IN YOURSELF!
HAVE FAITH IN
YOUR ABILITIES!

NORMAN VINCENT PEALE

WHY BE
normal
WHEN YOU
CAN BE
paranormal?

PRACTICE ANY ART... NOT TO GET MONEY OR FAME, BUT TO EXPERIENCE BECOMING, TO FIND OUT WHAT'S INSIDE YOU AND TO MAKE YOUR SOUL GROW.

KURT VONNEGUT

Either you run
the day or the
day runs you.

JIM ROHN

WHEN YOU BECOME
THE IMAGE OF YOUR
OWN IMAGINATION,
IT'S THE MOST
POWERFUL THING YOU
COULD EVER DO.

RuPAUL

YOU'RE
SUCH A
marvel

WATCH WITH
GLITTERING
EYES THE
WHOLE WORLD
AROUND YOU.

ROALD DAHL

I DON'T WANT OTHER
PEOPLE TO DECIDE WHO
I AM. I WANT TO DECIDE
THAT FOR MYSELF.

EMMA WATSON

IMPOSSIBLE
ONLY MEANS THAT
YOU HAVEN'T FOUND
THE SOLUTION YET.

ANONYMOUS

Do what you
were born to do.
You have to
trust yourself.

BEYONCÉ

Other people's opinion of you does not have to become your reality.

LES BROWN

I WISH I COULD
SHOW YOU... THE
ASTONISHING
LIGHT OF YOUR
OWN BEING.

HAFEZ

WE MUST NOT
ALLOW OTHER
PEOPLE'S LIMITED
PERCEPTIONS
TO DEFINE US.

VIRGINIA SATIR

YOU'RE
unbelievable

IF YOU DON'T
LIVE YOUR LIFE
THEN WHO WILL?

RIHANNA

THAT'S THE
THING WITH
MAGIC. YOU'VE
GOT TO KNOW
IT'S STILL HERE,
ALL AROUND
US, OR IT JUST
STAYS INVISIBLE
FOR YOU.

CHARLES DE LINT

THE UNIVERSE
BURIES STRANGE
JEWELS DEEP WITHIN
US ALL, AND THEN
STANDS BACK TO SEE
IF WE CAN FIND THEM.

ELIZABETH GILBERT

YOU'RE
wicca'd

WE HAVE TO DARE
TO BE OURSELVES,
HOWEVER FRIGHTENING
OR STRANGE THAT SELF
MAY PROVE TO BE.

MAY SARTON

Live boldly.
Push yourself.
Don't settle.

JOJO MOYES

YOU'RE
wand-erful

FIND OUT WHO YOU ARE AND BE THAT PERSON... FIND THAT TRUTH, LIVE THAT TRUTH AND EVERYTHING ELSE WILL COME.

ELLEN DeGENERES

WE KNOW WHAT WE ARE, BUT KNOW NOT WHAT WE MAY BE.

WILLIAM SHAKESPEARE

I don't
think limits.

USAIN BOLT

YOU HAVE
TO BE UNIQUE,
AND DIFFERENT,
AND SHINE IN
YOUR OWN WAY.

LADY GAGA

WHATEVER YOU
THINK YOU CAN
DO OR BELIEVE
YOU CAN DO,
BEGIN IT. ACTION
HAS MAGIC, GRACE
AND POWER IN IT.

JOHANN WOLFGANG VON GOETHE

ALWAYS GO WITH
YOUR PASSIONS.
NEVER ASK
YOURSELF IF IT'S
REALISTIC OR NOT.

DEEPAK CHOPRA

I don't
want realism.
I want magic!

TENNESSEE WILLIAMS

NO MATTER HOW
IMPORTANT EVERYTHING
ELSE IS TO MAGICAL
SUCCESS, BELIEF IS
THE MOST CRUCIAL.

DOROTHY MORRISON

SQUAD
ghouls

THERE'S NOTHING
MORE BADASS
THAN BEING
WHO YOU ARE.

DARREN CRISS

BELIEVE IN YOUR
HEART THAT
YOU'RE MEANT
TO LIVE A LIFE
FULL OF PASSION,
PURPOSE, MAGIC
AND MIRACLES.

ROY T. BENNETT

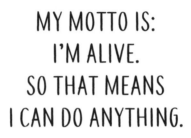

MY MOTTO IS:
I'M ALIVE.
SO THAT MEANS
I CAN DO ANYTHING.

VENUS WILLIAMS

Power means happiness: power means hard work and sacrifice.

BEYONCÉ

THERE'S NOTHING
MORE INTOXICATING
THAN DOING BIG,
BOLD THINGS..

JASON KILAR

YOU'RE

magi-cool

It's kind of
fun to do the
impossible.

WALT DISNEY

IT TAKES
COURAGE
TO GROW UP
AND BECOME
WHO YOU
REALLY ARE.

E. E. CUMMINGS

IF YOU SET YOUR
MIND TO SOMETHING,
YOU'LL ACHIEVE IT.

SARAH HYLAND

MAGIC EXISTS.
WHO CAN DOUBT
IT, WHEN THERE
ARE RAINBOWS AND
WILDFLOWERS, THE
MUSIC OF THE WIND
AND THE SILENCE
OF THE STARS?

NORA ROBERTS

TRY NEW THINGS.
DON'T BE AFRAID.
STEP OUT OF YOUR
COMFORT ZONES
AND SOAR.

MICHELLE OBAMA

EVERYTHING YOU DO **spells** SUCCESS

YOU NEED TO BELIEVE
IN YOURSELF AND WHAT
YOU DO. BE TENACIOUS
AND GENUINE.

CHRISTIAN LOUBOUTIN

To me,
a witch... isn't
afraid of facing
challenges.

PAULO COELHO

BOSS
witch

YOU ARE VERY
POWERFUL, PROVIDED
YOU KNOW HOW
POWERFUL YOU ARE.

YOGI BHAJAN

Be yourself.
An original is
always worth
more than
a copy.

SUZY KASSEM

THE POTENTIAL FOR GREATNESS LIVES WITHIN EACH OF US.

WILMA RUDOLPH

Dazzle
THEM WITH YOUR
divine self

YOU ARE
NEVER TOO OLD
TO SET ANOTHER
GOAL OR TO DREAM
A NEW DREAM.

LES BROWN

THE SHELL CAN BREAK BEFORE THE BIRD MUST FLY.

ALFRED, LORD TENNYSON

WE ARE
ALL MADE OF
=*stardust*=

IT AIN'T WHAT THEY
CALL YOU, IT'S WHAT
YOU ANSWER TO.

W. C. FIELDS

IF YOU CAN BELIEVE
SOMETHING GREAT,
YOU CAN ACHIEVE
SOMETHING GREAT.

KATY PERRY

People may
doubt what
you say, but
they will believe
what you do.

LEWIS CASS

WE DON'T KNOW WHO
WE ARE UNTIL WE SEE
WHAT WE CAN DO.

MARTHA GRIMES

Doubt whom you will, but never yourself.

CHRISTIAN
NESTELL BOVEE

I'VE GOT

99

problems,

BUT BEING A

witch

AIN'T ONE

I'VE NEVER
UNDERESTIMATED
MYSELF, THERE'S
NOTHING WRONG WITH
BEING AMBITIOUS.

ANGELA MERKEL

WE DELIGHT IN
THE BEAUTY OF THE
BUTTERFLY, BUT
RARELY ADMIT THE
CHANGES IT HAS
GONE THROUGH
TO ACHIEVE
THAT BEAUTY.

MAYA ANGELOU

NOTHING IS
IMPOSSIBLE. THE
WORD ITSELF SAYS
"I'M POSSIBLE!"

AUDREY HEPBURN

I FINALLY UNDERSTAND THAT MY BODY IS A MIRACLE.

AMERICA FERRERA

The way you
carry yourself
is influenced
by the way
you feel inside.

MARILYN MONROE

BE
FOREVER
magical

You were born
with wings. Why
prefer to crawl
through life?

RUMI

I WAS ALWAYS
LOOKING OUTSIDE
MYSELF FOR STRENGTH
AND CONFIDENCE,
BUT IT COMES FROM
WITHIN. IT IS THERE
ALL THE TIME.

ANNA FREUD

THE GREATEST DOER MUST ALSO BE THE GREATEST DREAMER.

THEODORE ROOSEVELT

YOUR AWESOMENESS IS some kind OF wizardry

WITHOUT LEAPS
OF IMAGINATION,
OR DREAMING, WE
LOSE THE EXCITEMENT
OF POSSIBILITIES.

GLORIA STEINEM

BE
UNAPOLOGETICALLY
YOU.

STEVE MARABOLI

YOU'RE SO
charming

IT IS CONFIDENCE
IN OUR BODIES,
MINDS AND
SPIRITS THAT
ALLOWS US TO
KEEP LOOKING
FOR NEW
ADVENTURES.

OPRAH WINFREY

The most
common way
people give up
their power is by
thinking they
don't have any.

ALICE WALKER

There is
real magic in
enthusiasm.

NORMAN
VINCENT PEALE

The
crystal ball
tells me your
future looks
bright

TO SHINE YOUR
BRIGHTEST LIGHT
IS TO BE WHO
YOU TRULY ARE.

ROY T. BENNETT

YOU'RE
magic

If you're interested in finding out more about our books, find us on Facebook at **Summersdale Publishers** and follow us on Twitter at **@Summersdale**.

www.summersdale.com

IMAGE CREDITS

pp.1, 2, 5, 9, 18, 26, 35, 39, 42, 50, 53, 61, 63, 74, 79, 88, 93, 102, 105, 109, 114, 119, 126, 130, 134, 140, 142, 148, 152, 158, 160 © Tatiana Kuzmina/Shutterstock.com

pp.3, 8, 12, 16, 21, 29, 37, 47, 49, 56, 67, 70, 75, 82, 84, 91, 95, 99, 107, 112, 121, 123, 133, 137, 149, 151 © Tamiris6/Shutterstock.com

pp.4, 15, 23, 32, 40, 51, 60, 71, 78, 86, 100, 113, 124, 138, 147, 156 © Alenka Karabanova/Shutterstock.com

pp.10, 20, 38, 48, 59, 66, 87, 101, 111, 118, 136, 143, 157 – crystal ball © Kate Cooper; sparkles © Tatiana Kuzmina/Shutterstock.com

pp.11, 22, 30, 36, 46, 57, 64, 72, 85, 96, 106, 116, 127, 135, 145, 155 © MaddyZ/Shutterstock.com

pp.13, 24, 34, 52, 55, 69, 76, 83, 104, 122, 129, 139, 150 © Giamportone/Shutterstock.com